HOW DOES A CAMERA WORK?
AF375475

HOW DOES A CAMERA WORK?

written by: Jennifer O'Brien
illustrated by: Ira Baykovska

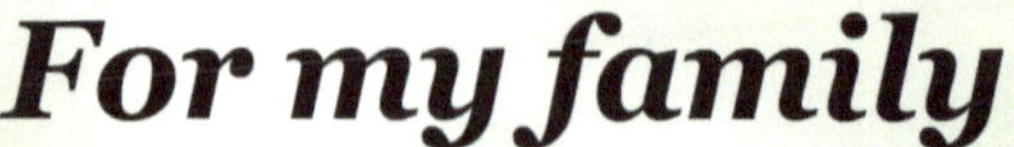

For my family

Copyedited by Brooke Vitale.

ISBN 979-8-9880623-4-9

NYC PHOTO PRESS
WWW.NYCPHOTOPRESS.COM

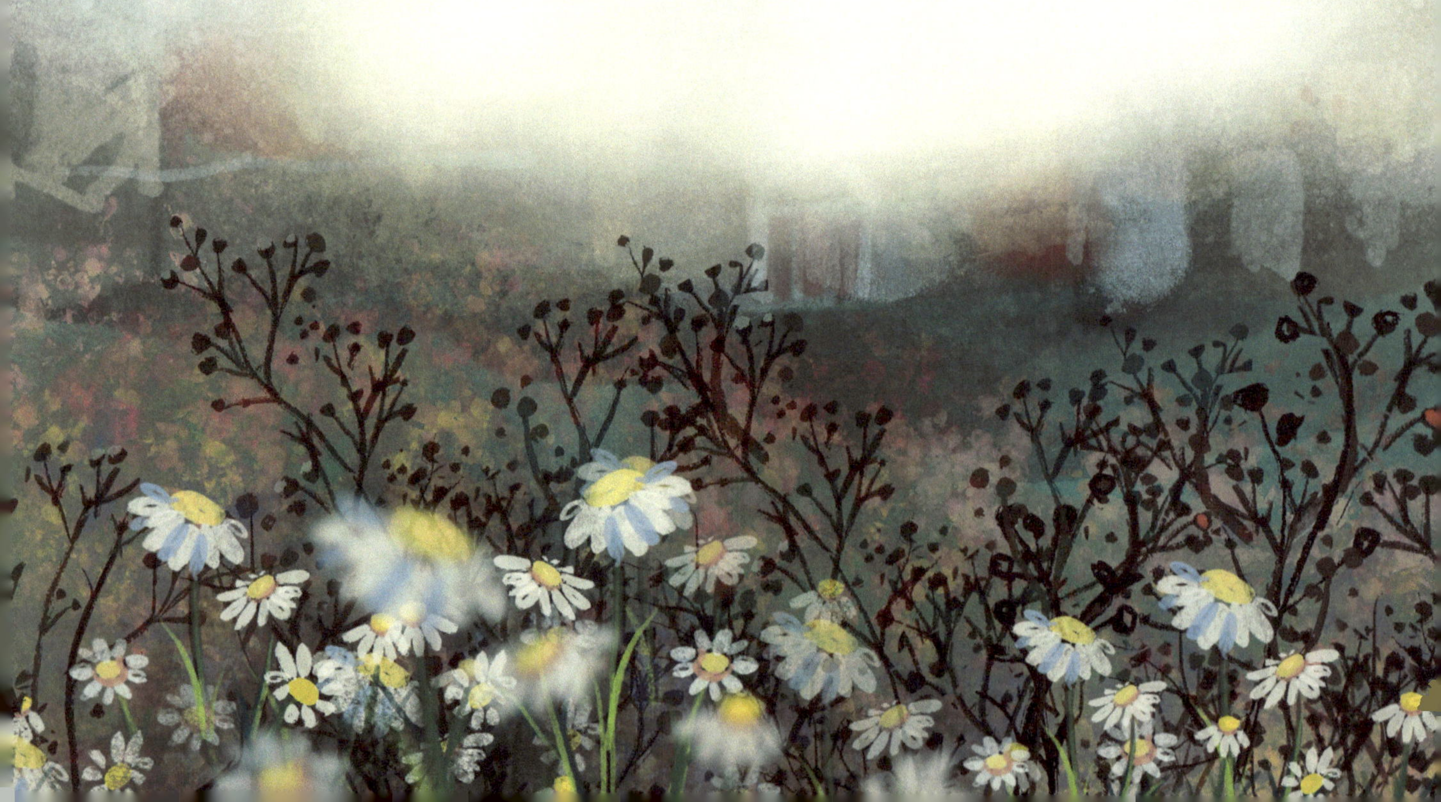

"Where is my camera?" Mom asked. Alex watched her mom, confused. Mom always has her camera. Always! Where could it be?

Mom scrambled through boxes
filled with film canisters and wires.
"Alex, have you seen my camera?
I want to bring it on our NYC trip!"

Alex shook her head.
"No, but can I ask you . . .
How does a camera work?"

"Great question!" Mom said.
"Cameras come in all shapes and
sizes, from a small phone camera
to a large camera with a long lens.
No matter what they look like on
the outside, all cameras look
very similar on the inside."

Digital Camera

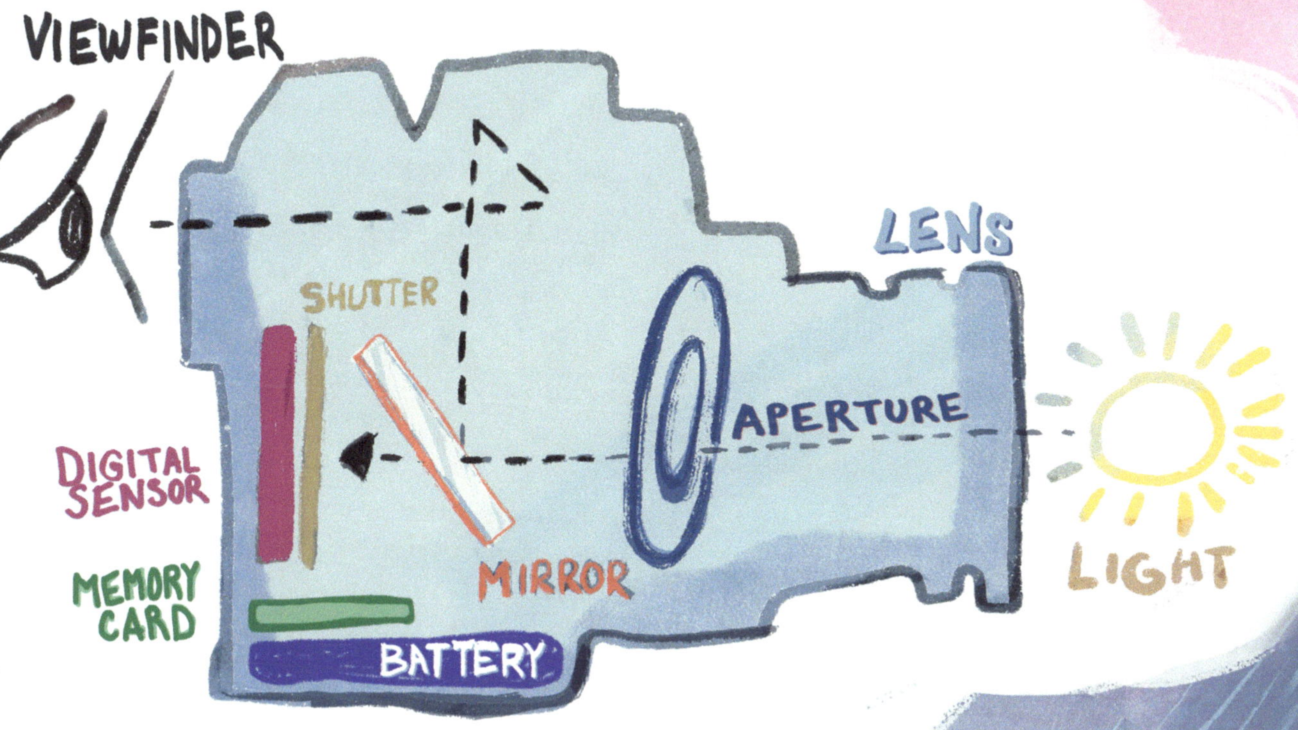

"A camera has a lot of moving pieces like the aperture and shutter that allow light in through the lens. I have two types of cameras. My film camera saves an image on film. My digital camera is powered by a battery, has a digital sensor, and saves an image on a memory card. A memory card could hold hundreds or thousands of photos."

"Is it like a mirror?" Alex asked.

"A little bit." Mom said, "it's a combination of a few things, but it does have a mirror inside. Well, mine does, anyway. Some newer mirrorless cameras don't have mirrors. Wait, I want to show you something." Mom raced out of the room.

Mom returned with a blue book of photos.

"Here are some of my favorite photos, including a self-portrait. I placed my camera on a tripod to play with the reflections in the mirror. Photography allows you to be creative and capture a moment in time so you can relive your favorite memories."

"Wow!" Alex smiled. "I see why you love your camera. Let's keep looking. I'll help!"

Alex spied something on the table.
"Mom, is a camera like a magnifying glass?"

Mom nodded. "Magnifying glasses are used to magnify or zoom into something. A zoom lens can do the same."

"If you zoom into just that part of the NYC skyline, you see the details of a building up close. Here's the Empire State Building from far away and zoomed in. Photographers like zooming in because it lets them be more creative. It changes the composition of a picture, or what you see in the frame of the photo."

"You can also choose how to hold the camera. A vertical 'portrait' photo is great to capture a person or tall buildings. A horizontal 'landscape' photo works well for a long bridge or group of people or buildings."

Alex was getting tired.
Soon, she started rubbing her eyes.
"Oh, is a camera like an eye?"
Alex yawned.

Mom explained, "Yes, they both have a lens. A camera lens uses an aperture to let light in. That's like the pupil of your eye—the black center part. Both open wider when there's not enough light to see and close smaller when there's too much light. Aperture also controls how much is in focus. For example, a wide aperture of 2 means one subject like a person or camera is in focus and everything else is blurry. A small aperture of 22 allows almost everything to be in focus."

22
2

"So our eyelids close like a shutter!" Alex said.

Mom grinned, "You're absolutely right. They open and close when you blink to let the right amount of light in through the lens."

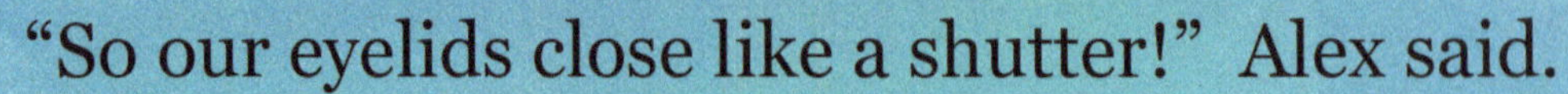

"If it's dark and the shutter is open longer, you can get a long exposure photo that shows the movement of water or taxi lights.

If the shutter closes faster, you can capture a specific frame of a speeding taxi or water droplets."

"I guess lots of things are like cameras,"
Alex said. "A mirror, a magnifying glass,
even my own eye!"

"That's right!" Mom exclaimed. "In a
camera, all those pieces work together. When
you click the shutter button, the light enters
the camera through the lens and aperture to
capture an image on the film or digital sensor."

PHOTOGRAP
TRAVEL
ART De
Empire S
Jen

Suddenly, Alex started smiling.
"You know what else is like a camera?"
she laughed. "Your camera! Look,
you left it on the bookshelf!"

Mom also started laughing.
"I can't believe it. I put it next to
the NYC books we were reading
to get ready for our trip!"

Alex scooped up the camera. "Can I take a photo?"

Mom nodded. "Of course, and I think I know the perfect thing to photograph!"

EMPIRE STATE BUILDING
Jennifer's Camera
NYC
Puglia ITALY

Glossary

Film canister:
a container that holds a roll of film used in a film camera

Film camera:
saves images on film, a roll of film might hold 24 or 36 photos

Digital camera:
has a digital sensor, saves images digitally on a memory card that
might hold hundreds or thousands of photos

Viewfinder:
the small window or screen you look through to preview a photo
before it is taken

Mirrorless camera:
has no mirror inside, uses an electronic viewfinder (screen)
instead of an optical viewfinder (window)

Composition:
what you choose to include in the frame of the photo

Tripod:
a three-legged stand that holds a camera steady,
great for a long exposure shot, video, or self-portrait

Self-portrait:
a photo you take of yourself

Portrait orientation:
hold a camera vertically to create a portrait photo

Landscape orientation:
hold a camera horizontally to create a landscape photo

Lens:
one or more pieces of glass where the light enters the camera

Aperture:
the opening that allows more or less light in through the lens

Shutter:
device that opens and closes, letting light expose the film/digital sensor

Long exposure:
a photo with a long shutter speed

Digital sensor:
captures the light required to form a digital photo

Memory card:
a chip that stores digital photos, videos, or information

Battery:
provides electrical power to the camera

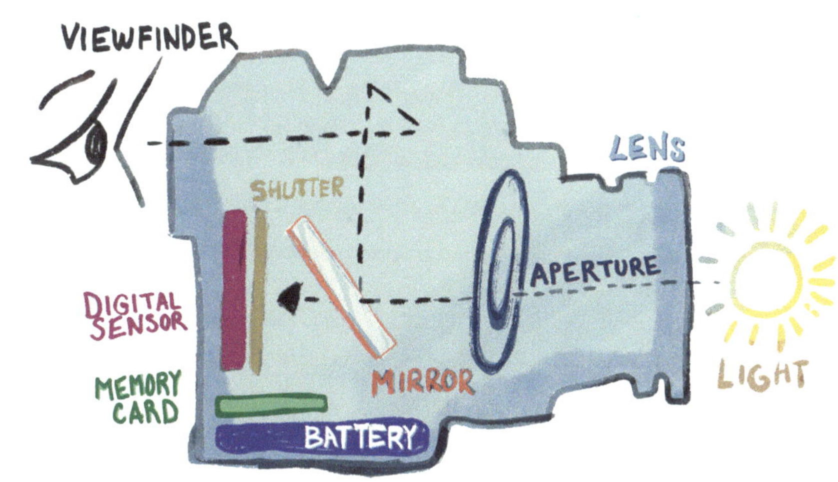